Overcoming You

Stepping Out on Faith to Create the Life you Want

Latoya T. Underwood

© 2018 By Latoya T. Underwood

Author Latoya T. Underwood
Independent Publisher
Latoyaunderwood@hotmail.com
Shutupandstrut@gmail.com

Overcoming You: Stepping Out on Faith to Create the Life You Want

ISBN 9781796683875

Printed in the United States of America. All rights reserved. This book or any portion thereof may not be reproduced or used in any manner whatsoever without the express written permission of the publisher except for the use of brief quotations in a book review.

ARD Book Services
Book Consultant
www.ardbookservices.com
345 Laverne Avenue, # Suite 14
Hillside, Illinois 60162

Over Coming You: Stepping out on Faith to Create the Life you Want

ACKNOWLEDGMENTS

I just want to thank God for giving me the idea to write this book. To help others step out on faith, take the risk, and live beyond mediocrity.

DEDICATION

This book is dedicated to first The Holy Spirit for giving me the desire to share my experiences. My parents Colvin Sr. and Angela Underwood. My family and friends Lynn Richardson and to anyone who desires to overcome their obstacles and reach their dreams! GO FOR IT!!!

TABLE OF CONTENTS

	Acknowledgments	iii
1	The Wall	Pg. 5
2	The Wilderness	Pg. 11
3	The Grasp	Pg. 13
4	The Approach	Pg. 19
5	The Step	Pg. 25
6	The Man in the Mirror	Pg. 29
7	The Vision	Pg. 35
8	The Faith	Pg. 43
9	Inspirational Closing	Pg. 47
10	About the Author	Pg. 49

1

THE WALL

It's Friday, January 25th in Chicago and it's 5 degrees below zero and gloomy. So cold the roads are white. So cold the wind literally takes your breath away... painfully. Yes cold.

The government has been shut down for weeks. At least four. When the shutdown began, we knew it wouldn't last any more than a few days let alone a week. However, like a slow paper cut the pain of the shutdown became unbearable. Eventually, everyone or someone we knew was affected. There was a silence in the air. A vibe, a mood... a different emotion. Friends who were strong the first two weeks of the shutdown began to break down. It was an eye-opening event. We literally had to "check on our strong friends."

In my opinion, this experience was a real wake up call for a few peers and me. To have something taken away that we expected every two weeks like a paycheck. Our livelihoods, our bread and butter and yet to have no power to stand or fight back. Today we're in bondage mentally, spiritually and sometimes financially. The choices we make result in us being tied up, chained and controlled. We overspend and live above our means or just simply want more in life. Which result in us working two or more jobs. Yes, including me.

Some of us chose to get in these horrible situations. Get it now and pay for it all later. Some of us are literally grinding our health away.

In life, we take so much for granted. We enjoy our clean water, food, shelter, our necessities, and even employment. But what if, it's taken away or the cost to consume it or live tripled. Could we afford it? Are we able to adjust and pay any increase? The question at hand is are you prepared?

Maybe we don't take everything for granted. For some of us, we are playing it safe. We work, eat, pay bills and thats enough for some. Let's not talk about a financial safety net or emergency fund. That's jumping the gun for some of us. But it is honestly needed.

If that's you and you're comfortable living as such that's fine, you have a right. I don't write to condemn or ridicule. I write to help you reflect and release. We all have our very own personal goals and dreams that require different work ethics.

Let's be real and transparent here my friend. Some of us are only comfortable because it's all you know. It's all you've ever seen. It's what we're accustomed to. Generation after generation some habits and struggles have become a way of life. Our generational curses are like a family secret. We know it's there, but we don't address it.

It's like we've build this invisible wall. A wall of silence. A wall that blocks opportunity. A wall that blocks vision. A wall that divides us from dreaming or setting goals. A wall where if you attempt to climb friends and family may judge you. A wall where we lack commitment and determination. A wall of lost hope! A wall where there is simply no FAITH!! However, every wall can be knocked down or crossed over. If you think you can you will. LET'S RENEW YOUR MINDSET TODAY.

Can you think of a situation where you felt like you were blocked by a wall? For some it can be a job. Deep inside you know there is something beyond the wall. More freedom, more pay, more time with your family and so on. However, you play it safe, you know this job pays just enough to cover your bills, the boss is a headache at times, but you choose to hang in there with hopes it will get better. I'm not saying quit your job. What I am saying is create ways to get over that wall. For example, maybe you can ask for a raise or you can STOP giving your boss the power of being a headache in your life. Bosses are human too, stop putting people on pedestals. Respect everyone BUT ONLY WORSHIP GOD.

Walls collapse when we address them instead of running away from them.

Let's begin to climb! There is SOMETHING inside of you reaching. We're reaching for something different. Something refreshing, something that's out of our norm. FRESH WATER!! NEW LIFE!! BETTER LIFE!! We desperately desire to leave the desert and pursue the LAND OF LIVING WATER.

Reaching for the rope of newness and hope. Yes,

it is easier said than done but its achievable!! And I'm sure you're sick and tired of being sick and tired!

Stop doubting yourself all the time. The moment you attempt to grab the rope, there is SOMETHING inside of us saying LET GO. It's too hard, I'm tired or I'm fine with the way things are. I can't do this. I don't have the resources. I'll do it when I get my money right. I have to pray about it. I'm waiting on God to move.

Even though, you're living in the wilderness you enjoy being here. I've been here for years. You're used to this struggle. You can't see or DESIRE to see pass the wall. My mother and my mother's mother struggled to dream. My father gave up the fight and so did his father.

I'll just stay here, play it safe and die right here. I love living in the dead. Dead marriage, dead business, dead career, dead family, dead finances, dead emotionally, just Dead Dead!!!

All dead situations lack FLOW! When a fish is alive, they swim against the stream, current or flow. A dead fish allows the flow to carry them wherever all the other dead fish land. Going against the flow takes work, strength and determination. It's a fight to flow. But the reward is LIFE!!

A dead marriage lacks the flow of love, joy, honesty and so forth! A dead business lacks the flow of creativity, network, ideas and cash. Are you living in the Flow? The overflow? Or are you just going with the flow of life, existing and barely making it? Settling? Dying slowly? Landing WHEREVER the flow takes you. Or are you fighting?

STOP using God as an excuse. Stop Saying you're waiting on God to Move, last I checked He is on the Throne and He's waiting on YOU!! SO, Let's Move!! Allow Him to Wake up the Lazarus situations in your life!!

THE WILDERNESS

Overcome the norm. Overcome the Generational Curses. Overcome the lack of knowledge. Overcome the COMFORT ZONES!!

My favorite Bible story is when God Promises the Children of Israel the City of Canaan. The spies visited the land to scope it out. However, when the spies returned some gave a report about the giants in the land. Deep inside they were afraid of change. Maybe they didn't feel qualified, but what we do know is they lacked Faith. They lack Perception. They settled for the Wilderness. It was safe. It was the norm. It was all they knew. Two of the spies, Joshua and Caleb had a different approach they saw the vegetables and fruit. They saw the potential. They trusted Gods promise. They were ready to do the work. They were excited about the land and wanted what was new, unfamiliar yet promised to them. A land of milk and honey.

Canaan was a land of possibilities! They saw the potential! They were willing to do the work and receive the BENEFITS of the PROMISE!

THE GRASP

Have you ever sat down or simply thought how could things be different for you? If you're like me I'm sure you've had those "What if " moments.

What if I left my hometown?

What if I saved more money?

What if I traveled more, got married early and so on? What if....

For years, I've always dream of moving away. Don't get me wrong I love the views, food and entertainment of Chicago. In addition, many of my family members are here.

However, the bitter cold and gloomy days can take a toll on a sister. And besides, who wants to stay in the same place forever? I will speak for myself.

Maybe this is why I love to travel. See different things. Experience tropical weathers and so on.

I always imagined living somewhere by the ocean. I find peace on the beach. There's a calmness and stillness that I enjoy. The clashing of the waves and birds singing gives me assurance like the voice of God. The sun set reflection on the water and the rhythm of the waves are truly the artwork of Him. Just to sit and watch the birds fly freely in the sky brings me joy!! I'm always in awe of God!

What does your dream destination look like? How does it make you feel? How does it smell? Yes, when you envision something, get in it! How does it feel, what sounds do you hear? What do you see? Smell and so forth! Imagination is a key component on stepping out on faith and reaching any goal.

Let's talk about money. Whew!! Let me be honest, as an entrepreneur I've wasted a lot of money, took risk and so forth! To God be the glory, I learned my lessons! He has allowed me to make it out of so many situations and jams.

Sometimes, I do wonder what if I saved more or

invested wisely? Well, I most likely wouldn't be in some of the situations I've been in. I also would travel the world more frequently. And invest in something like real-estate or another business venture. Do I regret my past NO! MY CHOICES? NO! And neither should you. I'm a firm believer that our past experiences make us who we are today. Every building has chips and cracks but they're still standing till this day! So Are You!!

Some consequences of the choices we made are painful. But we learned the lesson.... in some cases. Me being careless with money has actually resulted in personal conviction and now sacrifice. If I over spend foolishly, I'm INSTANTLY faced with conviction. Which leads me to sacrificing something. For example, if I over spend in a store. I now must cook every day for the upcoming week and or bring a lunch to work every day. Get it?

Let's be real here. Mistakes lead to consequences and consequences lead to painful memories. I really don't think it's a bad thing. The memories are a blessing. They will keep us on track. Unless we desire to repeat the same mistakes again. Think of the wall. It's up to you to keep climbing. Yes, there are days and seasons we all give up. WE ALL GET TIRED!! ITS NOT EASY! WE ALL HAVE MISSED THE MARK!!

You have to be determined to get over. We all have painful memories of the wrong choices we made but overcoming is always the goal.

Life is not about winning and losing. It's about winning and learning. I've learned so much about myself in my learning experiences. I'm sure you have too.

It's the pressure of life that has created the diamond in all of us!! Those challenges and obstacles where we might have fallen, got bruised but we didn't give up. It could be a marriage on the rocks where folks thought it was over. But your willingness to trust God and stay committed brought you through. It could be a business. As an entrepreneur and previous small business owner, there were many days where I wanted to quit and throw in the towel. Instead, God threw the towel back at me and said wipe the sweat off your face and keep going.

It could be a child that friends and family gave up on. BUT GOD! If we stay faithful and trust the process Anything can turn around, if it's in Gods Will.

Rest assured in knowing all seasons come to an end and there is a time for everything. Pray for wisdom. Everything isn't meant to be held on to. You must know when it's best to HOLD ON or LET IT GO. Yes, its ok to let somethings go.... release it.

My short testimony is "Honey I've been through the fire, but I don't smell like smoke." It's kind of funny but it's a true statement for me. I had to go through the Fire in order to Glow and Grow! My seasons of trails and reaping whether they were blessings or consequences, made me. I own it and I stand on it. MY BLESSINGS FOR BEING OBEDIENT AND SCARS FROM DISOBEDIENCE MADE ME. ACCEPT IT, FORGIVE YOURSELF, AND MOVE ON.

Stop beating yourself up. It's a new day, new grace, mercy and opportunities take hold and grasp the possibilities!! So many people are doing 180 degree turns in life. Turns of good, turns of blessings a turn into the overflow. Because they chose to stay committed to the will, the goal or the vision.

Take hold of your NEXT LEVEL! Release the doubt, fear and so forth! You can't hold on to both. Something has to go! The Spirit of Procrastination cannot reside with Execution!

Move or Sit, Live or Die! IT'S YOUR CHOICE!

There is a saying so many people die at 25 but are buried at 75.

Wake Up, Rise and Win!

THE APPROACH

I've got some Great News to Report!! Just in case you didn't know You're still alive! Ha!! Yes!!

There is still a chance to make it happen, all of it! From your residency, your career, or whatever you're trying to obtain! Approach it with a victorious mindset!

Each day we wake up is a new opportunity to reset! Resetting the way we live and change the way we think! Sometimes and most times we become stuck in cycles of life. We're afraid to attempt something new because of fear of failure and doubt. We're afraid of change and we don't want to leave others behind. Have the mindset of a leader not a sellout! You have to do what's best for you then reach back and show others the way. SOMEONE HAS TO DO IT, WHY NOT YOU? PEOPLE ARE DEPENDING ON YOU TO

WIN, THEY SECRETLY COUNT ON YOU!

Approach your goals differently. Approach your dreams as if there was an expiration date on them.

What if someone told you a year from today you would die. What would your response be? Would you panic and cry for 365 days? Or would you commit to living a fearless life? A life where you're unstoppable and doing everything you've ever dreamed or imagined? Would you PURSUE or become paralyzed? We're all going to die sooner or later, so LIVE YOUR BEST LIFE NOW!

The richest place on earth is the cemetery. There you will find dreams unfulfilled, books never created, business ideas that never took off and so forth. It's the land of would've, should've, could've but didn't. They never got around to it. Why? We will never know. However, what I can say is regret is a painful feeling.

Time, words and opportunities are things we will never get back. Sure, OPPORTUNITIES come back around but most times they never present themselves the same. They may come back later in life, after we've learned a lesson, loss, regret missing the previous opportunities and so forth. But never in the same moment in time. Don't let your dreams and goals die. If you did, then I strongly suggest you resuscitate them, at least one and try it again. Make another attempt. Pray and ask God to breathe on it!!

Your marriage, your children, family, business, finances and personal life may have been dead for years!! Ask Him to breathe life back into it! JUST ASK HIM!

Get the decay, callus, maggots and decomposition off your finances, family, your spirit and so forth. Yes, I know it sounds disgusting but that's the truth. When you're dead mentally, spiritually, you're no good to anyone. No one benefits from you. Your dead finances stink! Your marriage stinks! Your mindset stinks! It brings sorrow to those around you. No one can stand to be around you too long because it hurts seeing you in this situation. It's like seeing a friend tied up with rope and lock. You want to help your friend. However, your bound-up friend fails to realize the key to the lock is in their hand. Yes, the only way to get out of most situations is to realize we hold the key. I know it sounds tough but remember we're reflecting and releasing! The truth will set us free!!

Start where you are, use what you have and do what you can. Pick up where you left off!!

Get Over Your Setbacks and Obstacles!!! Stop thinking you're the only person who's experienced a loss or failure. It is not so. SURPRISE!!! YOU'RE NOT!!

Overcoming YOU, requires a mindset of VICTORY, NOT DEFEAT!! Giants fall at the sight of your faith!!! Begin to see where you want to be in life!! And work on a plan... a STRATEGIC Plan and work on getting there!!

Every plan sounds good, but a Great plan has task. For example, you can plan to lose weight. That's good. However, a greater plan to lose weight will consist of meal preps, exercise and so forth!! Example, you plan to take a trip to New York. Great, but how do you plan on getting there? Bus, train, plane or car? Will you uber or taxi from airport? Will you shop for local groceries or will you eat out each day? Get it?

Every goal we have needs a real plan. Yes, words are powerful but it's all in our actions and discipline.

Take a moment and jot down 3 goals you have this year.

This is your personal book, so be honest with yourself!

1) _____

2) _____

3) _____

Stop for a second, we all have different goals we desire to accomplish. I'm not saying go out and be a superhero. It's my DESIRE that you take a leap and do what you've always dreamed of. Go beyond your Norm! Ask God to help you Restore something that's broken!

For some, it may be the ability to take your entire family on a vacation. Pay your house off early. Start a business or write a book! What task are you willing to do or must do in order to reach your goal? What actions are you willing to take? What sacrifices are you willing to make?

Go for it! WRITE HERE

___

Stop delaying and get On Board!! Yes, there may be hiccups along the way. Plan it out anyway. If you fall off track... start over again or get an accountability partner.

A small change in direction or step is better than NONE.

It could be the hope of saving ten thousand dollars this year. YOUR GOALS AND DREAMS BELONG TO YOU!! It's all about being committed. Are you willing to stay dedicated?

5

THE STEP

Our next level requires a strategy, a plan, a task, willpower and strong commitment! Overcome what you're use to!! You have to step out to an unfamiliar place. Let me say it's scary at times but it's a beautiful place. COMFORT zones are deadly!!! We just discussed the Benefits of our Deadly Situations...Nothing grows there!

Deep down you may ask yourself why you? I'm here to reply, "WHY NOT YOU?" Someone is watching you, quietly and patiently waiting and hoping you win! Your perseverance means everything to them. Your mended marriage can inspire someone. Your decision to go back to school may encourage an onlooker. Your endurance to overcome pushes others to not give up.

Let's see the person you desire to become.

1) *Who do you want to become in 5 years? Are you working towards it?*
2) *SERIOUSLY, tell me all the details!*
3) *In 5 years, where will you live?*
4) *How much money will you make?*
5) *What places have you visited?*
6) *What other goals are you willing to ACCOMPLISH 5 years from today?*

See it's a process. Previously, I asked what 3 goals you are desiring to reach this year. But it's the decision we make this year, at this very moment that will reflect who we will become in 5 years.

1) *In 5 years where will you live?*
2) *What countries will you travel?*
3) *How much do you weigh?*
4) *What goals have you accomplished?*
5) *What's for dinner (yes, I need to know all the details)?*
6) *How much money do you give to charities yearly?*
7) *Are you a home owner or renter?*
8) *What else did I miss about you?*

See every detail big or small counts because that's exactly who you will become! Even who you associate yourself with plays a major role!!

If you're hanging around 4 doubters or naysayers soon you will be the 5th one. If your circle of friend's gossip, leave and ask God for NEW FRIENDS.

Influence is Everything!!

Now are you willing to put in the work? Honestly? Are you? You can fool me, but you can't fool yourself!!

What if I told you the length between your goals and your accomplishments are your ACTIONS!! ITS ALL IN WHAT YOU DO!! WORK YOUR FAITH!!

YES!!! Nothing works unless you WORK!! Yes, our actions and disciplined behavior is the ONLY thing separating us from our NOW to our NEXT!!

The Greater the Goal, The Greater the Work and the Greater the REWARD!

YOU CAN DO IT!!

An Olympic Medalist doesn't wake up 2 weeks prior to the Olympics and decide they want to compete. No!!! It takes intense training and SERIOUS sacrifices. You can't eat like you want, hang out and so forth and expect to live a VICTORIOUS LIFE!!! We REAP WHAT WE SOW!! IT TAKES WORK TO WIN AND KEEP THE GOLD MEDALS!

6

THE MAN IN THE MIRROR

As I write, God is showing me why He gave me this title OVERCOMING YOU. It's because " We get in our own way". Last year, I had to realize why I was in such a financial rut. It was because of the poor choices I made. I've experienced a foreclosure and lost 2 businesses not because of the recession but because I didn't adjust my spending. God provided all of my needs, but it was me who took His mercy for granted!! I knew WHO I wanted to become but my lack of preparation,

Commitment resulted in me losing what I had. I failed to downsize for a season. I knew I had to sacrifice somethings, but I refused. I refused to do the work. I refused to talk to the banks about my subprime mortgage. I began acting like the situation was invisible and that it would disappear eventually... and it did.

Honestly, this was a detrimental season of my life. I was embarrassed, ashamed and depressed. I opened my first business at 24, bought a condo at 25 and proceeded to open another business at 28. Everything was going well until I began making foolish mistakes. STRIKE I WAS OUT!! It seemed as if my world stood still and collapsed. Shutdown. This was truly a growing pain experience, but I made it through!! Thank you, Jesus! I made it through because I had to keep pushing. I fell and I laid down for about 4 years. Stuck, stagnant and back at my mama's house. To God be the Glory, I made it out! He was always there watching me like a Father watches over his children cheering me on. Just like a child may not win each time or make each shot but you cheer anyway hoping for a victorious outcome. The Holy Spirit was there encouraging, helping and listening always.

Unfortunately, there is a false teaching of prosperity that's overtaking our Media. Please believe and know if Jesus had to endure Calvary. You too will have life challenging experiences. I was cool about letting go the first business. I was cool about going to foreclosure court too. But when I knew the date, I had to leave the property and didn't have any money saved because I blew it, MY GOD!!! OR when the second business got slow, but payroll and rent were still due, God Take this cup from for ME! WHY AM I AM GOING THROUGH THIS!!! DECEMBER 2016, THE HOLY SPIRIT CONFIRMED TO LET IT GO! LET THE BUSINESS OF 8 YEARS GO!! BUT GOD WHY DID YOU ALLOW ME TO GO THROUGH ALL OF THIS?

In my heart, He simply said BECAUSE IT GREW YOU!

Yes, the last business was a Release Experience. When business got dead slow, I was doing all I could to hold on. So much so I was extremely depressed. I wasn't depressed to the point of suicide but I wanted to sleep the winter away. I recall being so depressed on the couch, our family dog Charlie sensed it. He just came and laid on my feet.

Today, people ask me why I closed. Only a few seem concerned, most just nosy. But I tell them why and I close with the words "I'M FREE"

That's because I am!! The pressure of that situation created the diamond I am today.

See if you want to Overcome YOU, step one requires you be honest with yourself. The moment you face and own up to your crazy behavior and struggles will be a moment of change. When you tell yourself ENOUGH of living in cycles, that will become your moment of SURRENDER. Some habits and behaviors have become generational. However, it can stop with You, if you face it head on!! Stop the blame game and throw the PRIDE out!! The moment you overcome you there is a peace and freedom that is SPIRITUALLY beautiful.

It's up to you to step out. The position we are in today is because of the choices we made yesterday. How long are you willing to stay here? That pain or emotion can be viewed as a scar, but it helps us become better stewards. Pain allows us to never forget. Some roads I never want to travel down again. Pain!

The remembrance of Pain can help us avoid making and creating something great including your future Life!!! Remember it's in the choices. Learn to overcome and break the routine. I know you're used to going out on the weekends. I look back and cringe thinking about all the money I've spent. One of my personal goals is to travel to

Africa and Dubai. Newsflash, I won't get there unless I become more Disciplined in my spending and saving. Right? Same for you, do the work and trust the process great things take Commitment!

No need to beat ourselves up. We know NOW! It's Now our hearts desire to live a fulfilled LIFE.

Remember the first step is being honest and realizing it is us that get in our own way.

We all have different goals and vision. Overcome you by doing what's good for you!!! Get out your own way! Stop competing and secretly comparing yourself to others. You will drive yourself crazy. Work, live and pursue your Dreams at your OWN PACE!

Overcoming You

7

THE VISION

To fully enjoy the BENEFITS of a Great LIFE you need peace! No matter what comes your way, you know in your mind everything will work out. Peace will work out. Peace comes from within. You will not and you will never find peace in material possessions. Cars, homes and fancy items are cute, but they are also billing. We've had enough bills to last a lifetime, well I have.

Peace is knowing you are enough. You are content with who you are at this very moment of life. Peace is trusting the process and Gods plan for your life. Trust me it's a process. Until you have mastered, embodied and experienced the power of Joy, Contentment and Peace, you will never feel or understand peace from within. You will constantly be searching for the next big thing, seeking fulfillment to no avail.

Once you are at peace with yourself and the

season of LIFE you are in then you can step out on faith and create the LIFE you want. Don't look back at life mistakes to feel bad. Only look back to see how far you've come. Now look forward at where you want to go. Overcoming You requires renewing your mindset and focus as often as needed. Yes, we all fall off. However, you must have a made-up mind to get back up!!! As a man or woman thinks in their heart. So is S(HE).

IT DOESN'T MATTER WHO THEY SAY YOU ARE. WHO DO YOU SAY YOU ARE?

I am QUALIFIED, an Overcomer, a Winner, A Giver and Leader.

Below write 5 Adjectives that Describe you!!!

1) _____

2) _____

3) _____

4) _____

5) _____

Yes, it's who you say you are that matters! Now let's step out on Faith! It does not matter what your goal is. It could be a family, business or health related. I've created 5 steps that will help you obtain it! All 5 steps my help your business and maybe 2 will help with your family. But they will help. The key is for you to apply them. Be sure to write notes between each step.

Step one: One must EVALUATE. What is the goal? Or what do you desire to accomplish? What will it cost me? What must I do in exchange to get it, to attain it? What are the benefits of this dream? How much is this dream worth?

Step two: You must now ELIMINATE. Since your dream will cost you something you will have to give up some people, places and things. Some people need to go. Write the initials of people names or places and things you need to ELIMINATE here:

_____

_____

_____

_____

_____

_____

Imagine taking a plane ride. The more luggage you have the more you have to pay. Your next level requires you to travel light. EVERYONE simply can't go. Yes, you love them, but they are weighing you down. Stop going places that don't resemble your future self. Remember, birds of a feather.... flock together. Here's a tip to cut off people. Simply get busy. The more they invite you and the more you say you're busy the less they will invite you out. Its ok. Some people are for a lesson and season. Once you ELIMINATE or Detox Get ready for Takeoff.

Step three: You need to EDUCATE yourself!! I don't care how good you are at something. Things are constantly changing. We perish from a lack of knowledge. Overcoming you requires wisdom. Educate and become the expert. Education increases your value. Get out of your way and learn something. Don't be a know it all. List 3 things you need to do to overcome and level up. Example, take a credit or money management class, attend a prayer or Bible class, workout class, whatever it may be list it here!!! Deep down we all know what we need. STOP RESISTING AND LIST IT!

Step four: ENGAGE. Creating the life you want requires being around those who resemble the life you want. Get out and network. There are people willing to connect, help, teach and mentor you! Let go of pride. Every new season of life will require some new associates!! Especially those who have done what you are trying to do!! It could be a married couple at your church that you and your spouse look up to connect and learn from them. Or a coworker who you want to mentor you.... List an organization you may need to join this year. For Example, my church and local chamber of commerce have played a great part in my development!!

Step five: If you want to Create the life you want. You have to create the life you want!!! Execute! That means do the work!! A cake never bakes itself. You need to have some money, drive to the store, go buy ingredients, prepare and serve!! You could also buy a cake already made but it will never taste or feel the same. Do the work, be proud of what it has become. Stop PROCRASTINATING and let's Get it done!!! Use this space just to free style and write.

Stepping Out on Faith to Create the Life You Want

8

THE FAITH

Overcoming you and stepping out on faith will not be easy but it will be worth it!!

Be at peace with who you are. Every situation, trail and obstacle has made you the person you are today. Get out of the way. There is SOMEONE inside of you trying to be free. He or she is banging to get released. But you are holding on because you're COMFORTABLE or you're afraid of the unfamiliar possibilities. Think of a butterfly. During the cocooned season maybe, you doubted yourself. You were afraid because you didn't want to leave your home. You faced rejection so you're COMFORTABLE staying in.

But now it's time to overcome and conquer. Overcome and be free!! Overcome the war and welcome some peace.

OVERCOME LOOKING AT THE GIANTS AND SEE THE GRAPES. Overcome and conquer. Overcome and be free!! Overcome chaos, HELL and the wilderness. Open your life, your children's life, your children's children's life to the possibilities and OPPORTUNITIES of SOMETHING BETTER. A life of fulfillment, hope, victory, a life of chances. Break down the wall of doubt, procrastination, rejection and fear. Shatter the glass ceilings with your faith and tenacity!! Keep pushing, Keep PRESSING!! YES, IT HURTS! YES, YOU'RE SACRIFICING!! YOU'RE TIRED BUT KEEP GOING! Set YOURSELF Free!!! Don't look Back at the giants, look forward at the GRAPES. OVERCOME YOU. Crawl, walk, run or jump!! But know and understand this is a daily process and there are numerous levels and stages. To overcome simply means to have SUCCESS over a problem or difficulty. Life is full of them, daily. It is up to us to look the other way, ignore it, or step up to the plate and accept the challenge.

Have the same Faith Peter had for a few seconds? Faith to step out the boat and walk on water. Faith where it seems impossible to others but if you keep your eyes on God it can happen.

Faith that says, even though I'm in a storm I can make it. Faith that says while everyone is sleep or playing it safe, I can do it!

So, go ahead, stop looking at your shortcomings. Overlook them! Step out on faith! Ask God, TRUST Him and walk it out! Overcome YOU!!

Conclusion

MY INSPIRATIONAL SUMMARY

So, what do you really want? Remember we all have different desires. It could be something as simple as using all your vacation days. A road trip, a book, business venture whatever. Its precious, it belongs to you but how long will you stall? Tomorrow is not promised to any of us. Within the 6 weeks I wrote this book I've lost 4 people that I knew personally... Yes 4 in 6 weeks. This inspiration is simply a plea. Don't take life or the luxury of time for granted. Embrace the possibilities of a new day! New grace and mercies. Take a moment each day and just meditate and thank God for what you do have. Ask Him what's next. We have wasted so much time doing things our way and as a result we're living in the wilderness. Going in circles and cycles like the children of Israel. Overcome you! God isn't checking your bank account. He is checking your faith account. If your faith account is insufficient or low well unfortunately you are playing it safe. Trust God! He always keeps His promises and His plans are for us to PROSPER not harm you. You can do it!! Break the cycles. IF God is the Creator and you're His Child, then it's in You!! Create what you want according to his will! Seek Him, trust and watch everything fall into place.

10

ABOUT THE AUTHOR

Since the age 11, Latoya Underwood always knew she wanted to become an Entrepreneur. It wasn't the money or status that attracted her. It was the freedom and creativity. At age 15, she created in her family basement a little salon called Napz2Buttaz. Looking back, the name makes anyone chuckle including me. However, it was something she created, was proud of and actually had a few clients here and there. Latoya always had the heart to serve others. Later she eventually opened a hair salon and later a clothing boutique. Her experience as an Entrepreneur for 18 years gave her the gift to wow people. She's has learned so much in BUSINESS from management to marketing. Currently, Latoya is helping other Entrepreneurs win in their businesses. Running a business can be stressful for anyone. She stands on the scripture, "We perish from a lack of KNOWLEDGE." That's exactly what she's doing helping others flourish and not die.

To obtain copies of this book please send your request to:

www.amazon.com

OR

LatoyaUnderwood@hotmail.com
Shutupandstrut@gmail.com

Latoya Underwood is also available for speaking engagements and entrepreneurial seminars.

You can also check out a few of her business eBooks at Payhip.Com/Shutupandstrut.

ARD
Book Services

A Publishing Company

A Special Shout Out To All

Special shout out to all of my close friends and family members. You all are dear to my heart. To my church family and coworkers who inspired me, thank you. My clients at the salon who are always supportive and encouraging me... yessss, thank you! Photographers, Mike Teague and Shanel Romain, thank you. Anyone who took time to attend my numerous events, your support means a lot. To my Entrepreneur peers who understand me, thank you. James Humphries for the referral. My girl with the soft spoken voice, heart of gold and who sat with me Monday after Monday, Aletha Doggett thank you. And finally, to the special client who overheard me tell someone about this book. You proceeded to tell me how shy you were and I interrupted to say "Girl stop being so shy, you can do it too" I meant it. You can do it Too!! Overcome You.

To God Be the Glory

Amen

Made in the USA
Middletown, DE
08 October 2021